Contents

Arctic Hero

by

Catherine Johnson

Illustrated by Seb Camagajevac

First published in 2008 in Great Britain by
Barrington Stoke Ltd
18 Walker Street, Edinburgh, EH3 7LP

www.barringtonstoke.co.uk

This edition published 2008

ISBN: 978-1-84299-652-2

Printed in Great Britain by Bell & Bain Ltd

Chapter 1
Two Lives

This is a true story.

It's a story about trekking across the wide frozen Arctic, fighting snow blindness and frost-bite. It's about facing the risk of starving to death or drowning. It's about getting to the North Pole before anyone else.

But this is also a story about one man, Matthew Henson, who lived two very different lives.

In one life he was just another black man who lived in the United States 100 years ago. At that time, many people still remembered what slavery was like, and America was still a country where blacks and whites lived apart. Matthew Henson did a lot of jobs that didn't pay very well. He washed up dishes in a café, worked as a porter on the railway, and ended up as a clerk in a government office. He worked hard all his life and died aged 88. He was buried with other poor people in New York City.

In his other life, the life out on the ice, this man was a hero. He was one of only a few Americans who could speak the language of the native people of Greenland. They were called the Inuit and their language was called Inuit too. Matt trusted them and learnt from their way of life. He was one of the most respected Arctic explorers of his time. He spent a lot of time there and knew the people well. His design for dog sleds is still in use.

Even today, 100 years later, the Inuit people of Greenland still sing songs and tell tales of 'Matt, the kind one'.

He was the first man to set foot at the North Pole. He's an American hero now. Matthew Henson. To his friends he was plain Matt ...

Chapter 2
Growing Up

Matt Henson was born near Washington DC in America in 1866. Slavery had only just been abolished in the USA in 1865 and though they were now free, black people's lives were still very hard. At that time they really were looked down on as second-class citizens. They could not use the same shops, or go to the same schools, or live in the same part of town. Even though Matt's parents had both been born free they were very poor. In many

of the states of America blacks and whites were forced to live apart by law.

By the time Matt was eight both his parents had died. Matt was raised by a step-mother who beat him often. The last time she beat him, Matt was so badly hurt he couldn't get out of bed for three days. Matt decided he couldn't stay with his step-mother any longer. Even though he was only just 11 years old, Matt ran away from home.

Matt went to the nearest big city, Washington DC, where he worked in a place called 'Janey's Home-Cooked Meals Café'. In those days it was quite common for a child of Matt's age to have a job. He washed up and cleared the tables and the owner, Janey Moore, gave him a place to sleep. She treated him a hundred times better than his step-mother, and Matt was grateful and worked hard for her. Matt was happy here for a while, but he was young and wanted some adventure. He didn't want to spend his whole life in a café.

One of the people who came often to Janey's Café was a sailor. Everyone called him Baltimore Jack. He told tales of the sea and travel to other lands. In those days the only way for a poor boy like Matt to see anything of the world was to work on board a ship. So, aged 12, Matt walked the 40 miles from Washington DC to the city of Baltimore on the coast and looked for a place on board a ship.

Chapter 3
The Katie Hinds

Life on board a ship in those days was hard work and sometimes cruel, and Matt could easily have had more beatings and hardship. But Matt was lucky. He was taken on as cabin boy on a ship called *The Katie Hinds*. The captain was a kind man called Captain Childs. Captain Childs could see Matt was quick to learn, and he took time to teach him reading, writing and maths.

In those days they had no computers, SatNav, or GPS (the system that marks your exact position anywhere in the world on a computer screen). Sailors had to guide their ships across huge seas using only the angles of the stars and planets. Captain Childs taught Matt navigation and astronomy as well. By the time he was 15, Matt had worked his way up from cabin boy to the post of Able Seaman. He was a trusted and hard-working member of the crew.

Going to sea then was very different to travel these days. In fact setting sail was more like blasting off into space. There were no radios, mobiles or telephones. A ship might be at sea for months at a time with no way to contact shore. Crew members had to rely on each other and everyone had to work together.

The Katie Hinds sailed all over the world. Matt crossed the Pacific and the Atlantic

Oceans. He sailed across the China Sea. He went as far north as the Arctic Circle. He saw icebergs and tropical islands and met all sorts of people. They spoke Spanish and Russian and Chinese and Arabic. He learnt a bit of as many languages as he could and as many different skills as possible – carpentry, sail mending, cooking, and basic medicine.

When Captain Childs died, Matt left *The Katie Hinds*. He was still only 17, but he had seen more than most grown men might see in a lifetime.

But back on shore in America, Matt was just another black teenager who needed a job. And there wasn't a lot of choice. Matt worked in the docks in Boston, loading and unloading ships. Then he got a job in a hotel, fetching and carrying for the guests. He moved around from Boston to New York and then back to Washington. It's easy to imagine that Matt wanted more out of his life.

Chapter 4
Meeting Robert Peary

Matt was 19 and was working in a big store in Washington when he first met Robert Peary. Robert was a Lieutenant in the American navy. He had come to the shop to buy tropical gear for his trip to Central America. There he planned to map out the path of the canal that was to be built linking the Atlantic and the Pacific oceans. He was also looking for a personal servant, or valet, to go with him.

Matt jumped at the chance to go travelling again.

Robert said later that he had been impressed with Matt. He had done so many different jobs and travelled round the world. Even though Matt was over 10 years younger than Robert, he had been at sea for many more years. And Matt could see that Robert was very keen to get on in the world and that he wanted to be a great explorer. Robert had already travelled to the frozen north of Greenland and hoped one day to return. Matt knew that, as a black man, this was something he would never be allowed to achieve on his own.

There was one more thing too. Robert showed a great deal of respect to Matt. For a white officer to treat a black lad this way was very rare. Matt could tell that Robert was someone he could work with. It was the beginning of a partnership that would last for more than 20 years.

The trip to Central America can't have been an easy one. The expedition had to hack its way through dense tropical jungle. This area was famous for its deadly swamps. People often died of malarial fever here. But Matt was a hard worker. He was skilled at wood-work and could make just about anything, if he had the tools. His years on board ship had made him a great team member.

Robert could see that Matt was too useful to remain as a servant – he was skilled at so many trades, he was strong and trustworthy, and he always worked hard. It was not long before Robert promoted him to join the team that was mapping the route of the new Panama Canal. Matt would never again be employed just as a servant to Robert.

But when the expedition was over Matt ended up back at the department store in Washington. It was a difficult time for Matt. It seemed as though his life was slowing down.

And then Robert sent a message from the Navy Yard in Philadelphia. He had found a job for Matt as a messenger boy. It wasn't much, but it meant a change of scene and a chance to work with Robert again.

Robert told Matt he was planning a trip north – he wanted his name to go down in history. Robert Peary wanted to be the first man to set foot at the North Pole.

Chapter 5
The First Trip North

The North Pole exists on the floating ice cap at the top of the world. To get to it, explorers have to travel across the sea ice for miles. Because there is no solid land underneath the ice, there are many dangers. What looks like solid ice can be just a thin crust of snow over a huge drop. This is called a crevasse. There are also 'leads'. These are areas of open water, like rivers, that flow through the ice. These can open suddenly, cutting off men from their camp and making it impossible to go on until the leads freeze over again. It can be as cold as minus 35 degrees. It can feel even colder in a snowstorm.

At this time, at the end of the 19th century, explorers from all over the world were racing to be first to get to the remote places in the world. Men from Norway and the United Kingdom were in just as much of a hurry as Robert and Matt to get to the North and South Poles. In some cases the race to the Pole would be a race to the death.

In 1891 Matt set sail with Robert and his crew. Their aim was to cross the northern tip of Greenland and explore this unknown land. Robert wanted to find out if it would be possible to cross the ice to the North Pole from the top of Greenland.

One of the crew was a man named Frederick Cook, who said he was a doctor. The others were scientists or men looking for adventure. Some of them paid to go with Robert, others were picked for their useful skills. Matt knew he wouldn't get paid, but he wanted something more than money. He wanted to be an explorer.

Their ship, *The Kite*, set the explorers down on the cold Greenland shore, just below a glacier, a solid river of ice. The ship would come back for them in a year. They had taken everything they would need with them except for dogs to drive the sleds and furs which they would buy from local Inuit tribes. They had to bring the wood for their huts and sledges, as no trees grew so far north. They took tinned food, including a mixture of meat and fat called pemmican, and biscuits, clothes and boots.

Chapter 6
The Inuit

Matt had never come across any Inuit people. The Inuit of Greenland lived the same way they had lived for hundreds of years, hunting and fishing. They knew how to survive even when it was as cold as minus 20 degrees and more. They wore animal furs to keep warm and were skilled at driving dog sleds. At that time, most people from Europe and North America thought of the Inuit as living in the Stone Age and didn't know anything about their way of life.

About three weeks after they had set up camp, Matt met some of the local Inuit people. The Inuit were interested in trade, selling dogs and furs to Peary's expedition in exchange for guns and other metal items like pots and pans. The Inuit had met Americans before, but they had never seen a black man. They were very interested by Matt, and they took him to be an Inuit. They could see that Matt was not a white man, so they thought he must be one of them.

Matt told them he was from a land far to the south, but he was happy to be welcomed and even happier to learn their language. Matt could see that it would be very useful to be skilled in the ways the Inuit hunted, travelled and survived. At this time, most 'civilised' nations thought that people like the Inuit were backward. But Matt knew that learning to survive in this harsh climate would be useful if he was to spend months at a time out on the ice.

One of the Inuit, Ahnalka, decided to be Matt's teacher and tutor him in hunting and sled driving. Matt found it easy to pick up the language – he'd been used to hearing so many on *The Katie Hind* that Inuit seemed to come easily. Ahnalka showed him how to drive a team of eight dogs and how to build a shelter, an igloo, from stone and snow. He showed him how to pack dry moss into the soles of his seal-skin boots to keep warm.

He also showed Matt how to warm up frost-bitten hands by holding them under your armpits. If your feet became frost-bitten, Ahnalka told him that the best way to deal with it was to warm your feet on a friend's bare belly. Frost-bite was a real killer in the Arctic Circle. The cold could cause your fingers and toes to freeze, killing and rotting the flesh. And frost-bitten limbs could get badly infected. Then you could lose your fingers or toes. Teeth, too, could fall out, the nerves frozen dead in your gums. And the

white glare all day and night could make you snow-blind.

Ahnalka also warned Matt that it was mad to go out onto the ice cap. Men could vanish into the crevasses just like that. And on this first trip one member of the team died, as Ahnalka had warned them. He vanished into a crevasse and his body was never found.

Matt had learnt a number of vital skills – dog driving, hunting and survival in the Arctic. This, plus his loyalty and hard work, meant that Robert could not do without him. As the years went by, he depended on him more and more.

Matt tried to teach the other members of the expedition sled driving and hunting. Frederick Cook, in particular, found it hard to work with the sled dogs. Matt soon saw that Cook had neither the patience nor the ability to work hard. You needed both for life on the ice. One time Frederick Cook insisted on going hunting with Matt and ended up scaring off a herd of reindeer they had tracked and followed for three days.

Matt and Robert later found out he wasn't a doctor – he'd never finished his medical training. Frederick Cook was in fact a milkman from a suburb of New York.

Chapter 7
The Next Trips North

Robert and Matt returned to the USA and planned a second trip the next year. The first trip had been a success and the Navy was now backing Robert's attempts to be the first man at the Pole. However the second journey ended in disaster. There were storms and the weather was colder than before – after one terrible storm the dogs' feet were frozen solid to the ice.

Matt and Robert didn't get to the Pole, though they did reach the furthest north recorded by man. But Robert had severe frost-bite. They had to send Ahnalka back to camp for help. Matt insisted he wanted to look at Robert's toes, but when he removed Robert's boots and socks, the blackened, rotten toes came away too. Robert lost nearly all his toes. If it hadn't been for the medical care Matt could give him, Robert would have lost his life as well.

Matt was so worn out by this trip he was close to death himself. Back at camp the Inuit fed him up with warm, freshly killed seal's blood. Robert couldn't bring himself to drink the seal's blood, and he took a lot longer to recover!

That set-back didn't stop Robert. He returned to the Arctic a year later and took back with him two huge meteorites, lumps of rock that had fallen there from outer space. He knew he would be able to sell them to

museums to raise money for more trips. He gave lectures about his expeditions, hoping for more money in order to make the final trip to the Pole.

Robert and Matt did, in fact, make three more expeditions between 1897 and 1902. They beat records for farthest north. They learnt how to pull loaded sleds across pressure ridges – frozen waves of ice. They survived frost-bite but they almost starved. They shot and killed their sled dogs when hunger grew too much. Matt almost lost his life when he fell into a crevasse, but was pulled out by Ahnalka.

****

But however hard life was in the Arctic, it was nothing compared to life in between these trips for Matt. He had been married, but the years away made it hard for his wife and he was divorced in 1902. Even worse was

the sort of work which he could do in America. Every time he came home he was reminded of his second-class status.

Out on the ice he was respected, skilled, important. At home in America all he could find was a job as a messenger boy. Matt made up his mind to try something else. He took a job as a porter with a big railway company. This was his chance – he thought – to explore his own country, and it was one of the best jobs open to a black man at the time.

Matt had grown up in the northern states of America, where things were less difficult for black people. What he saw in the South, in states like Georgia and Florida, shocked and horrified him. Black people were not allowed into white cafés and were forced to eat outside. Black people were often abused by whites even though slavery had ended 40 years earlier. One time Matt had to hide as night riders – a mob of violent white racists – came to take black men off the train to their death. Matt was abused and beaten by white men, and had to hold back from hitting back, as he would have lost his job – in fact, he would have lost everything.

He was just about ready to quit when a telegram came from Robert, who was planning a final trip to the Pole.

The public had grown tired of Robert's almost yearly attempts at the Pole and did not want to support any more expeditions. This might be their last chance.

Matt headed north at once.

Chapter 8
The Dash to the Pole

The ship was called *The Roosevelt* and she was an ice-breaker. Earlier trips had taught Robert that the further north the ship could break through the ice, the fewer miles they'd have to travel overland. And this time the crew were skilled men, not people looking for adventure. But there was a problem, well, more than one problem. It was said that Nansen, the most famous Arctic explorer, wanted to make an attempt to get to the North Pole. And Frederick Cook, the bogus doctor who had been with Robert and Matt on their very first trip, was already on his way north.

The Inuit people were always pleased to see Matt. They trusted him more than all the other explorers that they'd met. Matt never cheated them, Matt was still the only American who spoke the Inuit language and Matt respected them. The Inuit made sure Matt's expedition had the best dogs, the best furs, the best supplies they had to offer. The strongest Inuit were chosen to go with Matt and Robert. These men included Segloo and Ootah, two Inuit Matt had worked with before and had seen grow from children to young men during his years visiting Greenland. Matt was sad to see that Ahnalka wasn't with them as he had died some years before.

Robert had decided to plan this trip in a different way. He could not afford to fail. It was 1908 – he was 50 and Matt was 40. They were getting too old for exploration. And although he hated to admit it, Robert was almost a cripple after losing nine of his toes. He was forced to ride on a sledge most of the time.

They began sledging to the Pole in February when the Arctic winter was ending. This meant there was some daylight but the sea ice was still frozen. It was over 400 miles from the edge of land across the sea ice to the Pole. 400 miles of driving dog sleds through ice and snow and storms. On the way a 'lead' (a river in the ice) opened up, and the explorers had to wait for days before it re-froze and they could carry on with their journey.

Robert had planned that teams of men would leave stores and supplies for them along their route. Each team consisted of one American and two or three Inuit. They would go with Matt and Robert, their sleds laden with food, then leave the supplies at a marked depot before turning back. This way Matt and Robert would be able to pick up supplies on the way back, and not have to carry so much themselves.

Apart from Robert and his two Inuit guides, Eginwah and Ookeah, only one other team would go on the final push to the Pole. He had to choose who to take. Matt Henson had worked with Robert for 18 years. He had saved Robert's life and his skills made him the most important member of the party. He was even more important than the other white explorers, though they were all highly skilled men who had travelled widely. They were scientists, sportsmen, or sailors. They all knew Robert would pick Matt, though each of them would have liked to go to the North Pole, no one was surprised when he chose Matt. Ootah and Segloo would be the two Inuit to make up his team.

It was a hard trip, but they did not face as many problems as in their earlier expeditions. The weather held. There were no week-long snow storms or warm spells that might have made the ice crack or open. They made good time, even though Matt and Robert were worn out by travelling 18 miles a day.

Matt nearly died when his sled cut through thin ice over a lead and he fell in. He felt the freezing water like knife blades as it seeped through his furs. Then he was gripped and pulled down by the current, and it was only the swift action of Ootah, one of his Inuit team, that saved his life. Ootah pulled Matt free and changed his boots, and warmed Matt's frozen feet on his belly.

On the 3rd of April it suddenly became much colder. Matt was worried about how this would affect the ice. His team marched 20 miles a day for the last two days. Nothing

was going to keep him from the Pole this time.

It was Matt's team who made it to the Pole first on the 6th of April 1909. Matt knew they'd arrived when his compass went wild – suddenly there was no north for the arrow to point to. The midnight sun was high in the sky – up here, one day and one night was a whole year. Suddenly there was no north, only south, east and west.

Matt told the Inuit he was with, Ootah and Segloo, that their hunt was over. Robert and his team, Egingwah and Ookeah, arrived 45 minutes later. Robert made more readings and confirmed their position. It was difficult to take exact readings in the freezing air but Robert was as sure as he could be that they had reached the Pole.

They made camp and built an igloo, but the explorers spent only 30 hours at the Pole,

even though it had taken them 18 years to reach it. Robert took photos of Matt and the Inuit with Matt holding the Stars and Stripes flag. They were sure that they were the first men ever to stand at the North Pole.

They were worn out when they returned to camp. Robert and Matt had lost pounds in weight, but they had reached the North Pole which is what they had set out to do. Surely there would be a hero's welcome when they returned to America.

The Roosevelt took a few months to break through the ice and sail back to the port of Etah on the Greenland coast. When they arrived there in July they heard the worst possible news. Frederick Cook had left for New York in April, claiming that he had reached the Pole the year before, in spring of 1908.

Chapter 9
A Hero's Welcome?

Matt talked to the Inuit who'd travelled with Cook and they told him that Cook had never gone farther than 20 miles out on sea ice. Matt examined Cook's sledge, which he had left behind, and he could see it had been hardly used. Matt knew that Cook, who had pretended to be a doctor to get onto the very first expedition, was a liar and a coward. Matt also knew Cook was not very good at driving sled dogs and did not get on well with the Inuit.

He tried to tell Robert that it was so clear that Cook had made the story up that he would never be believed. But Robert knew that Frederick Cook was a very good liar. He had convinced the Explorers Club of New York that he had climbed one of the highest mountains in America, and that he was a doctor, when in truth he was a milkman.

It was Robert who turned out to be right. Cook had enjoyed crowds waving flags, and grand dinners with rich people of New York. He earned thousands of dollars from selling his story to newspapers. By the time Robert and Matt arrived in New York he was already touring round Europe, telling kings and queens all about his adventures and his courage out on the ice.

Cook told the public he had reached the Pole ahead of Robert Peary. And after all, how could Robert be trusted? Robert had taken a black man and a few Inuits with him, and none of them could possibly be trusted over the word of a white man.

Cook had no records and no scientific readings, and in the end he was thrown out of the Explorers Club. But even when it was proved that Cook was a liar, people were not ready to believe Robert. White Americans could not understand why any right-thinking man would choose to travel with a black man to the North Pole. It made no sense to them. Robert must be as big a liar as Cook, they thought. After all, his white companions were all sent back before reaching the Pole. Why didn't he choose to take one of them?

The books written about Robert at the time always made little mention of the part Matt had played. He was called "Peary's faithful coloured servant", when in fact, as one of Robert's team said, he was "of more real value than the combined services of the four white men on the team."

It took a year or two, but in the end Robert received the honours he deserved. However Matt, a "coloured man", was ignored. He spent a year or so on lecture tours of black universities (many universities had either all black or all white students) and local groups and he published a book about the trip to the Pole, but he needed a job with a regular income.

In the end, in 1913, he was offered a job in the Civil Service – working for the government. The job offer came in the form of a telegram from the President's Office. But it was only as a messenger boy. He was nearly 50 and he was a messenger boy. But Matt took it. It was better than parking cars, which was what he'd been doing while writing his book. He had married again just before the final trip and now had a wife to support.

His book, *A Negro Explorer at The North Pole*, made him a few dollars. (Negro or Coloured were the accepted words for African Americans at the time.) But Matt was not admitted to the National Geographic Society, nor to the Explorers Club of New York, even though Robert was President.

Robert died and was buried with full military honours in 1920. Matt was promoted from messenger boy to clerk in 1927.

Chapter 10
The Final Triumph

Things did start to change for Matt. In 1924 he was given the first of several honorary degrees from black universities. This did not bring in any money, nor was he accepted by everyone, but at least his achievement in getting to the North Pole was starting to be recognized.

As society started to change, Americans slowly woke up to what Matt had done. In 1937 the Explorers Club at last admitted him as a member, and in 1949, when Matt was 81, the United States Government gave him formal recognition of the part he had played in the discovery of the North Pole.

When Matt Henson died aged 88 in 1955, he had been formally thanked by the President, Dwight D. Eisenhower. But he was buried with other poor blacks in a local cemetery in a suburb of New York City.

In the 1950s and 1960s, the Civil Rights Movement began the long struggle towards equal rights for black Americans. It was then that all Americans began to learn about Matthew Henson. Matthew Henson was a man whose skill and dignity impressed all those he worked with, all those he met. A man that the Inuit of North Greenland still tell tales and sings songs about nearly 100 years later. A man with an Inuit name, Mahripaluq, which means 'the kind one'.

There are now colleges, sports halls, community centres, streets and buildings – even a United States Navy ship – named after Matthew Henson. In 2000, 45 years after his death, Matt was awarded the Hubbard Medal, one of the highest honours the American Government can give. TV programmes, magazine articles and books were made and written about the man who went from barefoot cabin boy to one of the most successful explorers of his generation, who became the first man at the North Pole.

One last thing. Matt and Robert spent years in the Arctic. It was discovered in the 1980s that Matt had a son. He lived with an Inuit woman during his years in the North after his divorce and before his second marriage. The scientist who discovered Matt's relatives, his son and grandchildren, took them to visit America in 1987. He showed them the graves of Robert and Matt. Robert's grave was huge, a massive stone monument in the Arlington Cemetery in Washington DC – where America's heroes are buried – carved with the words "The Discoverer of The North Pole". Then the Inuit visited Matt's grave in New York City. They could not understand why Matt, the man they admired most, was buried in a small local cemetery.

In 1988, Matthew Alexander Henson was buried again, this time next to Robert Peary in the Arlington Cemetery with full honours. Matt overcame poverty and racism to achieve more than most people ever will. He worked alongside Robert for nearly 20 years. They sledged across the ice cap and faced death side by side. 79 years after they made their last trip to the Arctic together the two men lay side by side.

Equal at last.

Postscript

Even today experts argue about who got to the North Pole first. As the North Pole isn't on land but on drifting ice, it would have been impossible for anyone to take exact readings from the stars and sun – the way Robert Peary and Matt did – to show the true site of the North Pole.

It is only in modern times that explorers have been able to know for sure where the Pole is. They use modern methods like GPS (Global Positioning System, a kind of SatNav which shows your exact position anywhere in the world on a computer screen). Because of this, most experts in the UK do not think that Matt and Robert made it to the North Pole. They think that the North Pole wasn't reached until 1969, by a British explorer called Sir Wally Herbert.

In the USA, many experts stand by Robert and Matt's accounts. They are sure that they did reach the North Pole.

In truth, the facts about where Matt, Robert and their Inuit team mates planted the American flag will never be known. But one thing all the experts agree on is that Matt and Robert's journeys in the Arctic showed amazing courage and great strength, not just of body, but of mind too. And Matthew Henson, the boy who ran away from home aged 11, was a true hero, and one of the greatest explorers of all time.

Barrington Stoke would like to thank all its readers for commenting on the manuscript before publication and in particular:

Lauren Allsopp

Emily Joy Barnsdale

Scott Driver

Nazia Forid

Oliver Hamp

Luke Johnson

Julie Loy

George Marshall

Tedmond Oputa

Megan Piper

Aamir Rawat

Jasmine Strickland-Scott

Andrew Tallis

Brigita Valaitis

Charlotte Webb

Molly Whittaker

Become a Consultant!

Would you like to give us feedback on our titles before they are published? Contact us at the email address below – we'd love to hear from you!

info@barringtonstoke.co.uk
www.barringtonstoke.co.uk

AUTHOR CHECK LIST

Catherine Johnson

What's the most dangerous journey you've ever gone on? And why?

When I was young I would travel across London on my own very late at night. I think the scariest journey was across my local park – London Fields – on my own at around three o'clock in the morning carrying a twenty-pound note.

Who would you least like to go exploring with?

A mouse. I remember taking one on the tube and it was very scared of the noise. Or my old headmistress, who I still have nightmares about.

Who is your hero?

Matthew Henson was incredible, brave and patient. He was a very rare and special kind of man. My own father and mother are really big heroes to me. When they married in 1954, marriages between black and white people were very unusual. My parents had to suffer all kinds of prejudice. People said it wouldn't last, that any children they had would be mad, bad, or troubled for life. That didn't happen, my parents were married for 38 years until my Dad died a few years ago. And me and my brother haven't done too badly in life.

Which country would you have liked to discover?

One where you can spend all day in your pyjamas with a cat on your lap and drink coffee, and where hoovering is banned.

ILLUSTRATOR CHECK LIST

Seb Camagajevac

What's the most dangerous journey you've ever gone on? And why?

A trip across the Atlantic to Los Angeles because I'm terrified of planes!

Where would you most like to explore? And why?

Antarctic. Because, not many people were there. And there are no mosquitos.

Who would be your ideal exploring partner? And why?

Matt Henson because he was resourceful, skilled and a hard worker.

Who would you least like to go exploring with?

My girlfriend, because she is very nervous when travelling longer distances.

Who is your hero?

My grandad.

Which country would you have liked to discover?

Australia or New Zealand.

Try another book in the
REALITY CHECK
series

The Land of Whizzing Arrows
by Simon Chapman

Pocket Hero
by Pippa Goodhart

The Last Duel
by Martyn Beardsley

Escape From Colditz
by Deborah Chancellor

Dick Turpin: Legends and Lies
by Terry Deary

Crazy Creatures
by Gill Arbuthnott

Mad Scientists

by Gill Arbuthnott

From the man who ate everything, to the cat that's both alive and dead ... welcome to the weird world of science!

"It's impossible to put down as each page reveals mind-boggling facts and spine-shivering details."
Amrita, age 13

Harald Hardnut

by Tony Bradman

The incredible true story of a feared Viking outlaw – bodyguard, soldier, killer, king – and hardnut!

"I liked it because it was an adventure and had fighting in it!"
Pratik, age 12

All available from our website:
www.barringtonstoke.co.uk